THE WESTERN ART OF
FREDERIC REMINGTON

BY MATTHEW BAIGELL

BALLANTINE BOOKS · NEW YORK

Art direction by Ian Summers

Book design by Ivan Paslavsky

Copyright © 1976 by Random House, Inc.

All rights reserved. Published in the United States by Ballantine
Books, a division of Random House, Inc., New York, and simultaneously
in Canada by Ballantine Books of Canada, Ltd., Toronto, Canada.

Library of Congress Catalog Card Number: 76-9744

ISBN 0-345-25128-8-595

Manufactured in the United States of America
First Edition: October 1976

For Caroline and Howard

THE WESTERN ART OF
FREDERIC REMINGTON

It is a matter of self congratulation that in ringing the final curtain on the great Wild West drama, the relentless course of empire has left us at least one auditor with skill and enthusiasm and courage enough to perpetuate on canvas and in enduring bronze the most inspiring phases of its colorful existence.

—Perriton Maxwell, 1907

I sat near the fire and looked intently at one human brute opposite. He was a perfect animal, so far as I could see. Never was there a face so replete with human depravity, stolid, ferocious, arrogant, and all the rest.... As a picture, perfect; as a reality, horrible.

—Frederic Remington, 1905

Frederic Remington at his home in New York.
Photo courtesy of Remington Art Museum, Ogdensburg, New York.

They made us many promises, more than I can remember, but they never kept but one; they promised to take our land, and they took it.

—Anonymous Indian

I

No matter how the settlement of the American West is interpreted, one fact stands out above the rest. Whites took the land away from the Indians.

One group of people displaced another. The ever-westward trek, organized, carried out, and completed within a single century by Europeans and white Americans, reached into lands revered and cherished by its inhabitants for countless generations. Through the nineteenth century, artists and illustrators recorded for posterity scenes characteristic of Indian life, the costumes and countenances of individual Indians, the beauties of the landscape, the awesome wonders of the high mountains, huge waterfalls, and endless deserts, and the westward advance of the white person's frontier. None portrayed the moving of that frontier and the meeting of the races upon it as graphically and as memorably as Frederic Remington, the best and certainly the most popular painter of the American West. Through his works contemporaries were able to glimpse the terrain, the people, and the kinds of experiences typical of that region. His enduring popularity, which began with his initial successes in the late 1880's, indicates that his are among the chief images by which subsequent generations visualized and, more important, conceptualized the western settlement.

The values and points of view he stressed were easily absorbed by the majority of Americans. These were depicted through scenes showing the rough, masculine life of cowboys on the frontier, the battles between soldiers and Indians, and the settlement of Indian lands by whites. These same values still appeal today, then as now based on certain assumptions unrecognized and unquestioned by the great majority of Americans. It was assumed that the land was free, available to whites, and, indeed, waiting to be taken and redeemed by them. Remington's paintings and illustrations reinforced these assumptions. If Hollywood

Westerns and dime novels are indications, few artists have ever had such a strong impact on the ways a country has read and continues to read its past history. Consequently, Remington's art is very important, not only for its fine stylistic qualities, but because it so brilliantly mirrors traditionally held notions of the westward migration. Remington's work teaches us about the past, and about our attitudes toward that past.

We identify Remington so thoroughly with the frontier and the early settlement that we sometimes forget he was born in 1861, only four years before Robert Henri, the leader of the Ash Can School, the first radical group of twentieth-century American artists. It is surprising to realize that Remington was only seven years old when the golden spike driven into the railroad tie at Promontory, Utah, signaled the completion of the first transcontinental railway. By the time he bought a sheep ranch in Kansas in 1883, that well-settled state was already leading the nation in corn production.

The frontier itself had ceased to exist years before Remington completed the vast majority of his paintings. In fact, some of his most interesting works date from the years and months just before his death in 1909,

at a time when significant numbers of young Americans were creating Cubist and Fauvist paintings in Paris.

Had Remington not died prematurely from complications brought on by an appendectomy, he might have lived long enough to know of the attack on Pearl Harbor.

On the other hand, he did travel to areas that had barely seen white persons. He camped out under blazing suns and in blinding snowstorms. He participated in military action against Indians in the Southwest, and he was very near Wounded Knee in the Dakotas in 1890 when the last major Indian uprising of the century ended in a disastrous massacre. Remington really did experience life on the frontier, but he often traveled to it in Pullman trains. As a result, many of his paintings were autobiographical, but at the same time they also evoked memories of the Old West. A contemporary chronicler as well as a historian, he created pictorial images of events that had either occurred in his experience or had passed and disappeared years earlier. His work runs the gamut from observed reality to nostalgic re-creation.

He loved the Old West, was fearful of the New, and helped create a romanticized image of the glory-days of settlement.

Along with men like Owen Wister, the most famous writer of western stories of the day, he helped fix in the 1880's the mythic image of the cowboy. Remington pictured him in his original guise as a rough, semibarbaric ne'er-do-well, but he also showed his transformation into a somewhat noble, hardworking, clean-living outdoorsman, the ancestor of the Lone Ranger. In Remington's paintings, realism amiably meshes with imagination. In his works the past still lives—as it actually happened and as many would like to think it happened. To the pleasure of some, to the anger of others, and in a paradoxical combination of these qualities to still others, Remington has created believable images of the Old West.

II

Born in Canton, in New York State, Remington developed an interest in art and a taste for the West at a young age. Robust as well as sensitive, he simultaneously explored rugged physical activities and artistic pursuits. As a student at Highland Military Academy in Worcester, Massachusetts, between 1876 and 1878, he often drew pictures of soldiers, desperados, Indians, and frontier scenes. It was not surprising, therefore, that when he entered Yale University in 1878, where he remained until his father's death in 1880, he both played on the football team and studied in the university's School of Fine Arts. This combination of interests, more common among American artists than one might imagine, also characterized the life-styles of George Bellows and Thomas Hart Benton. Like them, Remington belonged to that interesting and still underexplored category—the artist-athlete, rather than the artist-esthete. And like them, he seems to have mistrusted abstract art styles and ideas, and did not let them seriously impinge on his work.

The particular course of Remington's adult life was no doubt strongly influenced by his relationships with his parents. His father, a successful newspaper editor and political operator in northern New York State, must have seemed to him a mercurial figure. He fought in the Civil War and was absent from home during Remington's earliest years. When he returned, his son came to idolize him and responded enthusiastically to his stories of the war and of the camaraderie he had experienced in the military camps and in the western states. Remington may well have been particularly taken with the notion of imagining his father as a free spirit roaming at will in the world. By contrast, Remington's mother was down-to-earth, practical, even plodding, and was opposed to her son's increasingly serious interests in art. In rejecting the wishes and attitudes of one parent (his mother), Remington assertively developed particular interests and talents associated with the preferred parent—creativity, physical activity, a desire to meet and be with people, as well as a restlessness of spirit.

Be that as it may, Remington first traveled West—to Montana in 1881—not really to sketch scenes of western life, but, like other young men lacking particular business interests or training, to seek his fortune, perhaps in gold mining. He returned home empty-handed at the end of the summer, but shortly after he sold a sketch to Harper's Weekly. Although redrawn by a staff artist, its publication in the February 25, 1882, issue marked Remington's first appearance in a major magazine. Early in 1883 he headed West again, perhaps planning to settle there permanently. He tried several ventures, including sheep ranching in Kansas, but finding none to his liking he traveled further West in 1885 before returning east.

During these years of false starts and wide-ranging travels, he decided to become an artist. Deciding that additional study might be practical, if he were to make a living from his art, he enrolled in the Art Students League of New York in 1886. But the lure of the open country proved too strong, and after only a few months of school he left for the West once again. For the next decade these trips became annual forays. Over the years they provided him with the raw materials—sketches and photographs—to create some 2,750 paintings and drawings, and twenty-five bronzes. Wildly energetic, he also wrote eight books, one play, and a vast number of articles, and he assembled an extensive collection of western paraphernalia. His gold mine resided in his brushes and pens rather than in a land stake. As a result, he is remembered not as one of the lucky few who struck it rich but as the best of those who gave witness to the exploration, pacification, and settlement of the West.

His most important western trip was the one he took in 1886. Traveling in the Southwest, he joined a military unit searching for a small band of Apaches led by Geronimo. Following his return to the East, he sold virtually all of his sketches to Outing, a magazine edited by an old college friend. The affirmative public response to these illustrations prompted other editors to seek out Remington, and within a short period of time he rarely found himself without commissions or the prospect of sales.

By 1888 he had become one of the country's most popular magazine illustrators, catering to a seemingly unquenchable popular interest in the West. In that year, for example, sixty-four of his works were reproduced in The Century Magazine, fifty-four in Harper's Weekly, thirty-two in Outing, and twenty-seven in

A FIGHT IN THE STREET.
The Century Magazine, October, 1888.

<u>Youth's Companion</u>. Not satisfied with his blossoming career as an illustrator, Remington also sought recognition as an artist. As a consequence, during his free moments that year, he also created paintings meritorious enough to win two major prizes at the annual exhibition of the National Academy of Design. In subsequent years he held many one-man shows of his work, and magazines published reproductions of his paintings whether they illustrated particular articles or not.

But the fact remained—Remington was, first and last, an illustrator, although he tried bravely and with the encouragement of sympathetic critics to escape the pejorative connotations of that label.

In that subtle balance between content and composition, he invariably deflected the latter to enhance the former. And in that competition between pictorial values, such as texture and color relationships, and story line, he invariably assigned the latter the dominant role. In plain terms, when we look beyond the narrative sequences and the stylistic devices used to enhance them, there is little to hold our attention. But as an illustrator he was superb. We should now examine some of the techniques he knowingly or unknowingly used

to arrive at his position of continuing eminence. Some of them are superficial stylistic tricks; others touch profoundly on white American attitudes concerning the settlement and exploitation of the continent.

III

In Remington's day many people thought he portrayed the Old West honestly and truly. Men such as Owen Wister and Theodore Roosevelt, whose books and articles he illustrated, believed that future generations would understand the West through his works. These assessments are acceptable only if we agree with certain conventions of taste and cultural outlook of the time.

Most basically, Remington never questioned the right of whites to possess the land. His point of view was in total sympathy with the architects of Manifest Destiny—that somehow whites had a God-given right to settle

INDIAN SCOUTS ON GERONIMO'S TRAIL.
Cover of Harper's Weekly, January 9, 1886.

the trans-Mississippi lands and to run off anyone who tried to stop them. Rather than portray the Indians' majestic struggles to preserve what was rightfully theirs, Remington cast in heroic mold those who usurped their lands—
the explorers, mountain men, fur traders, soldiers, Indian agency employees, cowboys, and settlers, as well as their Spanish and French equivalents.

He often painted them responding bravely to Indian attack, while Indians were depicted as villains assaulting peaceful civilian wagon trains, innocent families, or outnumbered but stalwart soldiers. Our sympathies are always with the white invaders, never with the red defenders. Rarely, if ever, did Remington show soldiers burning Indian settlements, the indiscriminate slaughter of Indian families, or the many ways in which whites humiliated Indian men and women. In the drama of confrontation, Remington cast the whites in roles of nobility and virtue. He, like others, elevated the actual events to the level of a continuous morality play in which the forces of presumed good were inevitably shown to best advantage.

Remington easily accepted a self-justifying morality, and he evidently considered violence a solution to a problem rather than part of the problem itself.

This attitude appears to be basic to human nature, since it occurs in virtually all societies, but it has acquired special force in America, in part because of the American belief in the rightness of its goals and in, also, what America has presumed to be its special relationship with God. These twin notions can be traced all the way back to the Puritans. On a symbolic level the settlement of the West may also be viewed as a purging ritual in the nation's development, a test of its strengths and abilities, or as a way station on the road to the ultimate success of its beliefs through action. Whatever the means (violence and self-serving morality), the ends (possession of the continent) justified them.

But we cannot blame human nature or the Puritans for American violence and its particular brand of morality, nor should we say that ritualized violence (professional football, for instance) is a basic element in American culture without seeking further qualifications.

THE HEAD LAY IN THE WATER.
Harper's Magazine, June, 1894.

For during the years of Remington's initial popularity, Social Darwinism reigned in the world of business, and its postulates overflowed into the field of art. In brief, Social Darwinism applied Darwin's theories of evolution and survival of the fittest to business practices. Those who survived and triumphed were the toughest, the strongest, the most flexible, and the best able to cope with changing situations.

Among artists, Winslow Homer best projected these qualities, in his turn-of-the-century works. In seascapes, he juxtaposed roiling seas and rocky coastlines as if to emphasize the eternal conflicts between the earth's basic components, water and land. In his landscapes, hunting scenes, in which either the hunter or the hunted would survive, replaced earlier, amiable vacation scenes. Remington also painted scenes of conflict, but in less abstract ways. He pitted recognizable types against one another—cowboys and Indians, soldiers and Indians, or settlers and Indians. Or he showed humans fighting for survival against nature—in the desert-dry Southwest or in the storm-ridden winters of the plains and northern regions. In effect he domesticated the themes Homer portrayed abstractly, translating them into subjects more easily understood by the great majority of Americans. A painting of a mighty wave pounding against rocks by Homer did not (and perhaps still does not) convey the same immediacy of impact that resides in an Indian war party galloping around an encircled wagon train.

Remington even seems to have preferred themes of violence or competition when painting Indians in their own environment. His <u>Sun Dance</u>, for example, portrays one way in which Indian men were tested for bravery and stamina—by seeing how long they could remain conscious after their flesh was pierced with hooks.

Nor should we overlook the fact that most Indian battles—about 940 out of roughly 1,240—were fought after the Civil War. Armed encounters were simply more prevalent between 1870 and 1890, and illustrators like Remington undoubtedly responded to popular curiosity and public interest. By contrast, earlier western artists preferred to emphasize customs, habits, even landscape features, rather than warlike activities. Nevertheless, when the contest for land became more critical, painters clearly began to reveal in their works the escalating tensions between the Indians and the whites.

Given the attitudes of his time, Remington saw no reason to understand Indians.

Like Owen Wister and a host of others in literary, artistic, political, and scientific circles, Remington thought the Indians were an inferior race.

A bigot, he held in contempt virtually all social, racial, and religious groups other than those descended from northwestern European stock.

But in fairness to Remington, it should be noted that his brand of nativism reflected popularly held beliefs of the time concerning the supremacy of the Anglo-Saxon race.

the importance of mood, feeling, and suggestion as ways of conveying artistic meaning. By 1903, for instance, he could say that "what you want to do is just create the thought—materialize the spirit of the thing…then your audience discovers the thing you held back." But Remington never became a mystic, and it is doubtful that he

To his credit, Remington once admitted that he found the Indians' "peculiar method of thought" fascinating, although he countered his admission by saying "that no white man can ever penetrate the mystery of their mind or explain the reason of their acts."

Remington may well have adopted this attitude as a child of nineteenth-century scientism, according to which all things of the world were ultimately explainable through logic and reason. Mysterious processes of thought, of instinct, or of the imagination were concepts he may have associated with Indians and found inferior or irrelevant in the face of modern scientific thought. However, toward the end of the century a reaction to materialist and realist attitudes swept the art world; and Remington, perhaps aware of the new currents, modified his earlier beliefs, recognizing

would have ever appreciably changed his attitude toward Indians.

Mysticism and a positive interest in Indian cultures, however, characterized the young modernists early in the twentieth century. One can assume, therefore, that Remington would have responded unfavorably to their concerns had he lived longer. He probably would have been mystified by Marsden Hartley and Max Weber, who genuinely loved Indian art and culture and who were especially anxious to learn about the Indians' supposed easy access to unconscious and instinctive modes of behavior. These artists wanted to learn from the Indians rather than decry their ways, to use Indian lore as a way of coping with modern life rather than viewing the Indian as one of the problems of modern life. The gulf that opened between Remington and the younger painters firmly placed Remington on the retrospective side of American history, one that obviously still enchants so many people nervously looking back to a simpler past, evading a complicated present.

IV

Which past, and which West, are we talking about? From a chronological point of view there are many Wests—Indian, frontier, agricultural, urban, and industrial.

Remington preferred to paint the frontier West, the rough-and-tumble West that existed beyond the constraints of normal society.

He also enjoyed painting scenes of the early agricultural West, especially those which included cowboys and the first settlers—though he showed little interest in recording activities of farmers and townspeople. One senses that he disliked farmers more than he did Indians, since they heralded the end of the Old West, the West he really loved. He never painted the farmer as hero, nor did he portray a cowboy mending fences with the same fervor as one riding the range. Even Indians riding the open lands or engaged in other nondomestic activities were invested with a grace, dignity, and joy of life alien to his farming scenes. As far as Remington was concerned, prairie sod need never have been turned by a plow.

His reasons for preferring the Old West, the one he briefly experienced in the 1880's, are varied. He is reported to have once said: "I paint for boys, boys from ten to seventy." He really meant, in effect, that he painted for those who still wanted to believe in make-believe and for those who preferred strongly masculine, physical activities.

In truth, the Old West could only have been re-created through fantasy, through imaginative paintings. The frontier had closed in the 1880's, an event memorialized by historian Frederick Jackson Turner's brilliant essay of 1893, "The Significance of the Frontier in American History." Frustrated by the rapid disappearance of the Wild West, Remington stopped making extended trips across the western states and territories after 1895, explaining that the new brick buildings and the workmen erecting them spoiled his earlier illusions of the West. He was upset by the fact that the New West was forcing him to grow up, to face reality, and he would have none of it.

AN OLD-TIME NORTHERN PLAINS INDIAN—THE COUP.
Harper's Magazine, May, 1891.

But we can also read deeper meanings into his dislike of the New West. His cowboys, working as hired hands or engaged in ranch chores, look as if they lacked strength of character or will power. He seemed to suggest that wage slavery had robbed them of their masculinity. The virtues of self-reliance and psychological resilience sharply honed by constant unexpected adventure seemed to disappear with the arrival of range fences and newly planted rows of grain. Even his Indians lost their discernible inner poise when painted in Indian agency scenes.

By a curious leap of logic, Remington equated the loss of personal independence with a loss of Americanism. Self-reliance, physical sturdiness, and the ability to withstand the punishment of outdoor living became identifiably American, and particularly western, traits, according to Remington's way of thinking. He considered deviation from these characteristics to be unpatriotic and, somehow, to be associated with the new immigrants from southern and eastern Europe.

Furthermore, he linked such negative characteristics with the eastern United States.

What does all this mean? Remington considered anything less than the masculine ideal of physical strength as un-American; and he identified behavior appropriate to the Old West as being typically American. In effect, he set the Old West apart as a place and a state of mind different from other, more settled parts of the country and then called that section the most typically American part of the nation.

Why did he reason in this way? He wanted to keep his image of the Old West pure by blaming easily identifiable newcomers for its demise. He also wanted to stop time, to stop the flow of history, to prevent advancing civilization from swallowing up the Old West. This West fueled the fantasies of many people, especially those from the settled, domesticated East with its increasingly elaborate, industrialized society.

The Old West was for people like Remington an alternate society, a place to escape from the tight social strictures of the East. The charm of the Old West lay not in the ways it imitated the East, but in the qualities of life that set it apart. Above all it lacked refinement and civilization. It was not housebroken. It was savage. And, it was wonderful.

Remington lionized soldiers and cowboys in his paintings, though one doubts that he would have invited any to dine with him at his elegant home in New York or with his friends at a social club. In the Old West, however, everyone could live freely outside of societal constraints, call everyone "brother," and succeed or fail on the basis of his own merits—or so Remington seemed to suggest in his paintings and writings. The Old West was not so much a new Garden of Eden as it was a grand rumpus room, a place to which one could escape in mind and body. The Old West symbolized freedom and a true, pure, and uncomplicated America.

Remington was not the only painter to resent the encroachments of contemporary society. Thomas Cole, a leading figure of the earlier Hudson River School, lamented the arrival of the railroad into hitherto unspoiled valleys of New York State. Implicit in his observation was a nostalgia for what was passing away. Remington, too, was nostalgic

for what was dying in the Old West, and as the years went by he secluded himself more and more within his memories. He began to see himself as the recorder of the great saga of settlement rather than as an observer of current events. By 1905 he had convinced himself that during his first trip to the West in 1881, he had decided to record its passing into history. At that earlier time, speaking to an old man who had really experienced pioneer days, Remington later observed:

"I knew that the wild riders and vacant land were about to vanish forever—and the more I considered the subject, the bigger the <u>forever</u> loomed. Without knowing exactly how to do it, I began to try to record some facts about me, and the more I looked the more the panorama unfolded.... I saw the living, breathing end of three centuries of smoke and dust and sweat."

Remington appears to have let nostalgia take complete charge of his feelings about the Old West, for these are the words of a middle-aged man, not the thoughts of a twenty-year-old drifter. But whatever his motivations, paintings did in fact pour from his brushes, and succeeding generations are in his debt for the view of the Old West he did provide.

Remington loved the Old West in yet another way. He preferred spontaneous and human activities to self-conscious and abstract thoughts; quick personal responses to lengthy intellectual digressions. This does not mean that he rarely read books or that he was anti-intellectual, but that he felt more comfortable portraying events based on observable actions rather than on abstract processes of reasoning. He preferred, as he said, "men with the bark on." Furthermore, although not opposed to modern technological developments, he could not easily incorporate the kind of thinking they represented into his art. They did not suggest to him the immediate impact of the concrete occurrence, the experienced moment. For example, just before the Spanish-American War, Remington was aboard the battleship Iowa, cruising Cuban waters. Restless and frustrated because of the lack of action, he wrote the following account of the ship's men: "I believe they fairly worship this throbbing mass of mysterious iron; I believe they love this bewildering power which they control. Its problems entrance them; but it simply stuns me." Like other artists, such as Benton and Bellows, Remington responded best to direct human encounters. Together, their art reflects a wide-ranging and continuing American mistrust of abstract ideas, symbolized for Remington by the triumph of civilization over the Old West.

V

Few artists or illustrators have so neatly reflected and recorded the bigotry, love of violence, and desire for escape of their own and of subsequent generations. But having such a firm grip on the public's pulse does not alone ensure success. Such insights must be visualized, and Remington was one of the master American illustrators. No other painter of the western settlement has projected particular scenes or selected the right kinds and proper amounts of detail so well. Other artists and illustrators have confused the viewer with too much detail, diverted attention from the subject with extraneous figures, painted forms too woodenly, or selected a moment in the narrative that is not the most significant or easily grasped. Not so, Remington. Invariably he picked the right moment, and then by combining stylistic components with startling acumen, he manipulated the viewer into accepting the authenticity of the scene. It is surprising how easy it is to remember specific Remington paintings.

What were some of the techniques he used? As if to underline the fact that Remington's frontier was as much a product of his imagination as it was a real place, its topographical features are rarely defined.

BRONCOS AND TIMBER WOLVES.
The Century Magazine, January, 1889.

Remington's frontier really has no location. He usually indicated landscape features with schematically rendered details—some underbrush, a distant mountain. More precise definition of background details would have imposed reality upon the dream.

Consequently, his figures emerge clearly because there is so little background to clutter the view. It is as if a giant lawn mower had removed most of the plants and trees before Remington arranged his figures; only splotchy touches of pigment represent rocks, sand, or bushes. Throughout most of his career, Remington painted scenes at high noon. As a result, light clarifies rather than obscures forms. The viewer never has to wonder if he should look at the subject or at some wonderfully articulated purple shadow. Ease of understanding is emphasized above all else.

Remington concentrated his attention on people. He did not paint the grandeur of the West. Occasionally mountains shade off into vague distances, but in a typical painting the action takes place on a relatively shallow stage. The land is only a backdrop, it never competes for attention. As a result, Remington engages his viewers directly in the action shown. Precise renderings of form characterize articles of clothing as well as textures of animal skins and furs. Faces are clearly delineated. The figures, which so easily dominate the spaces they inhabit, take on mythic dimensions. One reads tremendous heroism in their activities because their size is immeasurable and untestable against the harsh but barely indicated landscapes. One wants to identify with them because they move so easily through space. And their space is a continuation of our own, since Remington wisely preferred eye-level to bird's-eye or snake's-eye views.

Furthermore, his figures are rarely sickly, mangy, or ragged. Although not always handsome, they usually project through their postures and general bearing a strength of spirit, a larger-than-life quality that makes fantasy identification between viewer and painted figure altogether too easy. This identification is further prompted by Remington's habit of painting average, hardworking individuals who on the basis of their own physical energy created the Old West. He rarely painted the generals, the chiefs, or the ranch owners. Egalitarian and democratic, his figures are male fantasy images, nameless and without any responsibility for making important decisions. They are strong of character but have few obligations to weigh them down. To Remington, cowboys were what gems and porcelains were to others, and he imbued them with a symbolic value that extended far beyond the immediate matter at hand.

One of Remington's most remarkable traits can be seen most easily in his battle scenes—his distinct unwillingness to show direct confrontations between opposing forces. He usually focused on attackers or on defenders, but rarely on the battle joined. Quite often he omitted one or the other group of adversaries so that viewers could concentrate on the attack or on the defense. In this way we can enter more easily into the spirit of the picture. If we are on the winning side, we are not encumbered by having to face down a particular enemy. We win, and we win clean. If we are among the defenders, we do not always know how badly we are outnumbered or how helpless is our position. Rescue, perhaps victory, becomes possible. Since we do not see the resolution—nor can we always determine it from the information Remington provided—we can invent any resolution our imaginations dictate. In many works, such as Old Time Plains Fight, we feel that those still living will somehow survive, since each of us—the boys between ten and seventy at least—can easily figure out a means to escape the otherwise hopeless situation.

One of Remington's great talents was his ability to show people in varying postures. His inventiveness of form is most evident in his multifigured compositions. In these, virtually every figure looks in a different direction, holds a different body position, and physically responds to something within his own range of perception. In A Dash for the Timber, surely one of his best works, the eight horsemen shoot rifles and revolvers, or cock revolvers, or help a wounded buddy, or simply gallop as fast as possible. And each horse has distinctive mark-

ings. In those paintings where nothing exciting is happening, Remington managed to invent many incidents that continually entertain the viewer. In A Cavalryman's Breakfast on the Plains, the group nearest the foreground sits and stands in different postures as if waiting for the coffee to boil; the second group appears to be still involved with its morning toilet; and a third group is reaching for food. In the background a soldier carries a bucket while another reports to an officer. Nothing happens, but there is considerable activity.

The sense of liveliness with which Remington imbued his figures was further enhanced by his manipulation of textures. He was not afraid to leave thickened coils of pigment on a canvas surface or to interlace one color into another so that, for example, a horse's flank or a pair of trousers was really composed of many distinct and separate brush strokes. His paintings contained few outlines—an unexpected trait in the work of an illustrator—but rather carefully edged planes or independent touches of color. In fact, some works of the 1880's and 1890's contain passages of pigment as rough and as sketchlike as one may find in contemporary American Impressionist paintings or in the works of Robert Henri's twentieth-century group, but never to the extent of confusing the narrative line.

The precise sources of Remington's style are still unknown, but certain assumptions can be made. His teacher at the Art Students League was J. Alden Weir, an Impressionist;

and Remington counted Childe Hassam, another Impressionist, among his close friends. Evidently, as his style evolved through the 1890's, his own predisposition to attack the canvas with rapid strokes was reinforced by their example. Around 1905, Remington started to experiment directly with Impressionist techniques, dabbing paint all over his figures, laying down different colors side by side, and making shadows in luminous blue shades. The actual colors of objects occasionally disappeared in a welter of blue, red, and yellow strokes. But he never became a full-fledged Impressionist despite the great importance he assigned to color differentiation; his years of practice as an illustrator precluded that possibility. Highlights and shadows still remained within the scale of the actual color of the particular object, and edges of forms, although blurred, never lost their ability to define precise objects. A horse, a cowboy, or an Indian still emerges quite distinctly from the painted ground. His was an applied Impressionism, in part a technique used to lift himself up from the ranks of illustrator to that of artist.

Nevertheless, he manipulated brushy techniques effectively to suggest, as he had said, "the spirit of the thing." The soft touches of color especially contributed brooding, mysterious qualities to paintings of night scenes, which began to intrigue Remington around 1900. As Remington's memories of the Old West grew more distant and as he became more and more a "studio" painter, he obviously enjoyed exploring the possibilities of pigment and of textural variations. But he may also have created some of his night pieces as special mementos to the past, since they appear to be archetypal views of the Old West. They represent typical experiences even if they lack precise story lines or anecdotal qualities. The coach in The Old Stage Coach of the Plains, for example, does more than merely move down a hill at night. By its central, elevated position and as the only object with bright colors, it assumes iconic significance. This is not just any stagecoach; it is the apotheosis of stagecoaches. It glides mysteriously, soundlessly, endlessly over the land or, more accurately, over the geography of Remington's memory. Surely in this work Remington paid homage to one of the primary vehicles of the western settlement.

In similar fashion he painted Indians sitting around a campfire, thus preserving on canvas an increasingly rare sight, or he portrayed hunters returning from the hunt at a time when settlements and towns had made the hunter obsolete. Certainly many of these night views conjured up memories of the lost days of the past and celebrated them in ways unavailable to the sharp light of high noon. These were fanciful re-creations, historical romances, whose magic would have evaporated in the sunshine. Drawn from Remington's memory, they are paintings that in their quiet ways allowed his fantasies to mingle with remembered facts and that still allow the viewer to wander off into his own fantasies. These are soundless pictures. They are pictures for dreaming.

VI

This quality of fantasy must ultimately lie at the center of Remington's general appeal. In the works of other painters of the West we look at figures performing specific actions. We keep a certain distance from them. In Remington's paintings we can slip easily into the roles played by the figures. But this easy identification implies acceptance of Remington's values. Whether we realize it or not, he tells us things about ourselves we do not always want to know.

A WHITE TRAPPER.
Harper's Magazine, May, 1891.

About the Author

Matthew Baigell received his doctorate from the University of Pennsylvania. After teaching at Ohio State University, he joined Rutgers University in 1968. He has directed the university's graduate program in art history, and, since 1971, has served as chairperson of the Rutgers College art department.

For a variety of journals, he has written articles on nineteenth-century American architecture and twentieth-century American painting. His books include: <u>A History of American Painting; The American Scene: American Painting in the 1930's; Thomas Hart Benton</u>; and <u>Charles Burchfield</u>. He edited <u>A Thomas Hart Benton Miscellany</u>. He is currently exploring the connections and continuities between traditional and radical modes of American art in the decades before World War I.

LIST OF COLOR PLATES

Frederic Remington

CAVALRYMAN (1887).
Collection of William Rockhill Nelson Gallery of Art, Kansas City, Missouri. Bequest of Katherine Harvey. Reproduction rights reserved.

INDIAN WARRIOR ON HORSE, FORT RENO (1888).
Courtesy of Kennedy Galleries, Inc., New York, New York.

A DASH FOR THE TIMBER (1889).
Courtesy of Amon Carter Museum of Western Art, Fort Worth, Texas.

AN INDIAN TRAPPER (1889).
Courtesy of Amon Carter Museum of Western Art, Fort Worth, Texas.

MEXICAN COWBOY ON HORSEBACK WITH TRAPPINGS (circa 1889).
Courtesy of Kennedy Galleries, Inc., New York, New York.

THE SCOUTS (circa 1889).
Courtesy of Kennedy Galleries, Inc., New York, New York.

A CAVALRYMAN'S BREAKFAST ON THE PLAINS (circa 1890).
Courtesy of Amon Carter Museum of Western Art, Fort Worth, Texas.

THE SCOUT: FRIENDS OR ENEMIES? (circa 1890).
Courtesy of Sterling and Francine Clark Art Institute, Williamstown, Massachusetts.

DISMOUNTED: THE FOURTH TROOPERS MOVING THE LED HORSES (1890).
Courtesy of Sterling and Francine Clark Art Institute, Williamstown, Massachusetts.

TURN HIM LOOSE, BILL (prob. period 1890–1895).
Courtesy of Kennedy Galleries, Inc., New York, New York.

THE FALL OF THE COWBOY (circa 1895).
Courtesy of Amon Carter Museum of Western Art, Fort Worth, Texas.

THE FIGHT FOR THE WATERHOLE (prob. period 1895–1902).
Courtesy of the Museum of Fine Arts, Houston, Texas. The Hogg Brothers Collection.

THE EMIGRANTS (prob. period 1895–1902).
Courtesy of the Museum of Fine Arts, Houston, Texas. The Hogg Brothers Collection.

AIDING A COMRADE (prob. period 1895–1902).
Courtesy of the Museum of Fine Arts, Houston, Texas. The Hogg Brothers Collection.

STAMPEDING WAGON TRAIN HORSES (prob. period 1895–1902).
Courtesy of The University of Kansas Museum of Art, Lawrence, Kansas. Gift of Dr. and Mrs. Hugo Emmerich.

THE HOLD UP (prob. period 1895–1902).
Courtesy of the Valley National Bank Collection, Phoenix, Arizona.

OLD TIME PLAINS FIGHT (prob. period 1895–1902).
Courtesy of Remington Art Museum, Ogdensburg, New York. All rights reserved.

THE QUARREL (prob. period 1895–1902).
Courtesy of the National Cowboy Hall of Fame and Western Heritage Center, Oklahoma City, Oklahoma.

THE OLD STAGE COACH OF THE PLAINS (circa 1902).
Courtesy of Amon Carter Museum of Western Art, Fort Worth, Texas.

THE COWBOY (1902).
Courtesy of Amon Carter Museum of Western Art, Fort Worth, Texas.

A NEW YEAR ON THE CIMARRON (1903).
Courtesy of the Museum of Fine Arts, Houston, Texas. The Hogg Brothers Collection.

HIS FIRST LESSON (1903).
Courtesy of Amon Carter Museum of Western Art, Fort Worth, Texas.

PONY TRACKS IN THE BUFFALO TRAILS (1904).
Courtesy of Amon Carter Museum of Western Art, Fort Worth, Texas.

RIDDEN DOWN (1905).
Courtesy of Amon Carter Museum of Western Art, Fort Worth, Texas.

THE SMOKE SIGNAL (1905).
Courtesy of Amon Carter Museum of Western Art, Fort Worth, Texas.

AGAINST THE SUNSET (1906).
Courtesy of Kennedy Galleries, Inc., New York, New York.

THE LAST MARCH (1906).

CAVALRY CHARGES ON THE SOUTHERN PLAINS (1907).
The Metropolitan Museum of Art, New York, New York. Gift of Several Gentlemen, 1911.

COMING AND GOING OF THE PONY EXPRESS (prob. period 1907–1908).
Courtesy of the Thomas Gilcrease Institute of American History and Art, Tulsa, Oklahoma.

THE GRASS FIRE (1908).
Courtesy of Amon Carter Museum of Western Art, Fort Worth, Texas.

SHOTGUN HOSPITALITY (1908).
Courtesy of the Trustees of Dartmouth College, Hanover, New Hampshire.

THE LONGHORN CATTLE SIGN (1908).
Courtesy of Amon Carter Museum of Western Art, Fort Worth, Texas.

IN FROM THE NIGHT HERD (circa 1908).
Courtesy of the National Cowboy Hall of Fame and Western Heritage Center, Oklahoma City, Oklahoma.

STAMPEDED BY LIGHTNING (1908).
Courtesy of the Thomas Gilcrease Institute of American History and Art, Tulsa, Oklahoma.

THE LAST OF HIS RACE (1908).
Courtesy of Yale University Art Gallery, New Haven, Connecticut.

INDIANS SIMULATING BUFFALO (1908).
Courtesy of the Toledo Museum of Art, Toledo, Ohio. Gift of Florence Scott Libbey.

WHEN HIS HEART IS BAD (1908).
Courtesy of Kennedy Galleries, Inc., New York, New York.

NAVAJO RAID (prob. period 1908–1909).
Courtesy of Newhouse Galleries, Inc., New York, New York.

COWBOY (circa 1890).
Courtesy of Kennedy Galleries, Inc., New York, New York.

EPISODE OF THE BUFFALO GUN (1909).
Courtesy of the Museum of Fine Arts, Houston, Texas. The Hogg Brothers Collection.

THE SUN DANCE (circa 1909).

THE GUARD OF THE WHISKEY TRADER (1909).
Courtesy of University of Arizona Museum of Art, Samuel L. Kingan Collection, Tucson, Arizona.

APACHES LISTENING (circa 1909).

HUNTER'S CAMP IN THE BIG HORN (1909).
Courtesy of Kennedy Galleries, Inc., New York, New York.

A CAVALRY SCRAP (1909).
Courtesy of the Art of the Americas Collections, The University of Texas at Austin.

THE OUTLIER (1909).
Courtesy of The Brooklyn Museum, Brooklyn, New York. Bequest of Miss Charlotte R. Stillman.